BEING HEALTHY
Grain Products

Heather C. Hudak

Weigl

CALGARY
www.weigl.com

Published by Weigl Educational Publishers Limited
6325 10ᵗʰ Street SE
Calgary, Alberta, Canada
T2H 2Z9

Website: www.weigl.com

Library and Archives Canada Cataloguing in Publication data available upon request.
Fax (403) 233-7769 for the attention of the Publishing Records department.

ISBN 978-1-55388-418-7 (hard cover)
ISBN 978-1-55388-419-4 (soft cover)

Printed in the United States of America
1 2 3 4 5 6 7 8 9 0   12 11 10 09 08

Editor: Heather C. Hudak
Design: Kathryn Livingstone, Terry Paulhus

We gratefully acknowledge the financial support of the Government of Canada
through the Book Publishing Industry Development Program (BPIDP) for our
publishing activities.

Contents

You Are What You Eat

Fruit & Vegetables
5–6 servings

Meat & Alternatives
1–2 servings

From the top of your head to the tip of your toes, you are what you eat. To keep everything working in top form, it is important to eat a balanced diet, drink plenty of water, and be active.

How do you decide what foods to eat? Do you have a special diet, or do you eat whatever you like? There are many guides, such as Canada's Food Guide, that can help you make good choices about the foods you eat.

According to Canada's Food Guide, there are four main food groups. Eating a certain number of servings from each of the food groups every day is one way to help keep your body fit. Healthy eating habits can help prevent heart disease, **obesity**, **diabetes**, and certain types of cancers.

Canadian Food Guide
Recommended Daily Servings for Ages 4-13

Milk & Alternatives
2–4 servings

Grain Products
4–6 servings

Food for Thought

Think about the foods you ate today. How do your eating habits compare to those of other people?

Only 50 percent of Canadian children aged 4 to 18 eat the minimum recommended servings of fruit and vegetables each day.

Thirty percent of Canadian children have at least one soft drink each day.

About 75 percent of children in Canada do not eat the recommended number of grain products.

In Canada, nearly 30 percent of children eat French fries at least twice a week.

Getting to Know Grains

All over the world, grains are a staple food. From the first meal of the day to the side dish at supper, you likely eat many grains each day.

Think about your breakfast this morning. Did you have a bowl of cereal or a slice of toast? These foods are made with grains. At dinner, you may have corn or rice with your meal. These are also grains.

Grain products are any foods made from grains such as barley, oats, rice, wheat, and corn. Some other foods that fall into the grain products group are oatmeal, pasta, and tortillas.

Types of Grain

Wheat

Barley

Rice

Corn

Oats

Food for Thought

Did you know wheat is the most common and useful grain in the world?

Wheat is called the "staff of life" because it has so many great uses for people in every part of the planet.

Gluten is a tough, elastic **protein** found in grain products. It makes dough sticky and bread chewy.

Only wheat has enough gluten to make a loaf of bread. It helps the bread rise before it bakes. Gluten also helps bread hold its shape.

Growing Grains

Grains come from wild grasses that are grown as crops.

Each grain plant has a stem, head, leaves, and roots. Seeds, or kernels, form inside the head. Kernels have three main parts. These are **bran**, **germ**, and **endosperm**.

head

stem

leaves

bran

endosperm

germ

Making Flour

1 Farmers plant seeds that grow into grains, such as wheat.

2 Special machines water the crop.

3 Once a plant has reached its full size and the kernels have dried, it is ready to harvest.

4 The harvested wheat is stored in large bins called silos.

5 Next the wheat is milled. This means it is cleaned using special machines.

6 Then, the grain is ground into flour. Flour is used to make foods, such as bread.

Whole Grains

Movies always seem a bit better if you have a tub of popcorn to enjoy while watching. Popcorn is a whole grain, and it is a great choice for a healthy snack, as long as it is butter free.

Whole grains keep their bran, germ, and endosperm intact. This is especially important because bran gives us the fibre our digestive system needs to stay healthy. Germ is filled with fatty acids and nutrients that our bodies need. Oatmeal, popcorn, and brown rice are examples of whole grains.

Whole grains are rich in **antioxidants**, **minerals**, **vitamins**, and protein. This can have major health benefits. To get the best results, make sure that at least half of the grain products you eat each day are made with whole grains. Magnesium is also found in whole grains. This mineral helps build strong bones.

Food for Thought

How can you tell if a food was made with whole or refined grains?

Many food package labels are hard to read. If the label says the item contains whole grain, whole wheat, or multigrain, it may not qualify as a whole grain product. Look for labels that say the food is made with 100 percent whole grain whole wheat.

Just because bread is brown it does not mean it has the health benefits of whole grains. Sometimes, molasses is used to give breads their brown colour.

Get the Facts on Nutrition
Learn how to read a food label

When looking for whole grain products, it is important to read the ingredient list on the food you are buying to check its nutritional value.

The Nutrition Facts table will include the list of **calories** and 13 nutrients.

Nutrition Facts

Serving Size 1 Cake (43g)
Servings Per Container 5

Amount Per Serving

Calories 200 Calories from Fat 90

	% Daily Value*
Total Fat 10g	15%
Saturated Fat 5g	25%
Trans Fat 0g	
Cholesterol 0mg	0%
Sodium 100mg	4%
Total Carbohydrate 26g	9%
Dietary Fiber 0g	0%
Sugars 19g	
Protein 1g	

Vitamin A 0%	•	Vitamin C 0%
Calcium 0%	•	Iron 2%

* Percent Daily Values are based on a 2,000 calorie diet. Your daily values may be higher or lower depending on your calorie needs:

		Calories:	2,000	2,500
Total Fat	Less than		65g	80g
Sat. Fat	Less than		20g	25g
Cholesterol	Less than		300mg	300mg
Sodium	Less than		2,400mg	2,400mg
Total Carbohydrate			300g	375g
Dietary Fiber			25g	30g

1 The facts tell you the serving size and the number of servings in the package. The size of the serving determines the number of calories.

2 Calories tell you how much energy you will get from a serving. Children who get at least one hour of exercise each day should eat between 1,700 and 1,800 calories every day.

3 The first nutrients listed are **fats**. It is important to limit the number of fats you eat each day.

4 The next nutrients listed are fibre, vitamins, and minerals. These are the parts of food that keep your body healthy and in great shape.

5 The % Daily Value shows how much of the nutrients you need are in one serving of food.

6 The information at the bottom of the label further explains the calorie, nutrient, and % Daily Value information.

Refined Grains

Think about your favourite book. Would it be as good if the main character were missing? Refined grains are missing the bran and germ from the kernel. These are some of the best parts of the grain. Bran and germ are important for helping your body keep fit.

When grains are milled, the bran and germ are removed. One benefit of milling is that milled grains last longer. However, they have fewer B vitamins and less fibre and iron. To help make sure that these grains still have value, most are enriched. This means that certain B vitamins and iron are added to milled products. Examples of refined grains are white bread, white rice, and pretzels.

Food for Thought

Why are iron and B vitamins important to your health?

B vitamins, such as thiamin, riboflavin, niacin, and folic acid, help the body release energy from fat, protein, and **carbohydrates**.

Iron carries oxygen in the blood. Without enough iron, your body may feel tired.

Whole Grains vs Refined Grains

Your body needs a certain amount of fats, carbohydrates, and protein to keep it powered. It is important to find the right balance. If a person eats 1,800 calories each day, about 203 to 293 grams should come from carbohydrates, 40 to 70 grams from fats, and 60 to 158 grams from protein. This chart shows the calories, carbohydrate, fat, and protein content of some basic foods.

Whole Grains	Refined Grains
Multi-grain bread with whole grain 69 calories, 1 gram fat, 11 grams carbohydrates, 3 grams protein	**White Bread** 80 calories, 1 gram fat, 15 grams carbohydrates, 2 grams protein
Whole grain brown rice 170 calories, 2 grams fat, 34 grams carbohydrates, 4 grams protein	**Long grain white rice** 150 calories, 0 gram fat, 35 grams carbohydrates, 3 grams protein
Whole wheat spaghetti 174 calories, 1 gram fat, 37 grams carbohydrates, 7 grams protein	**Regular spaghetti** 140 calories, 1 gram fat, 43 grams carbohydrates, 8 grams protein
Oats 20 calories, 0 gram fat, 4 grams carbohydrates, 1 gram protein	**Instant oatmeal** 105 calories, 2 grams fat, 19 grams carbohydrates, 4 grams protein

Since meals made with whole grains are healthier than refined grains, try making a sandwich with whole grain bread instead of white bread.

Get Up and Go

Like a car, your body needs fuel to keep it moving. Grains are filled with the type of fuel that can keep your body running.

Sugars and starches that are found naturally in foods are called carbohydrates, or carbs. Much of the energy you need to run and play comes from carbs.

What Are Carbohydrates?

Learn how your body gets the fuel it needs

Carbohydrates, or carbs, can be broken into two main groups, simple sugars and complex sugars. Simple sugars lack vitamins and are found in refined sugars, such as candies. Fruit and milk also contain simple sugars, but these foods have other vitamins that the body needs. Complex sugars are found in starches, such as grain products.

Your body breaks down carbs into simple sugars, or glucose, that are absorbed by the blood. As the level of glucose in blood rises, the **pancreas** releases insulin. Insulin helps move glucose from the blood to cells. Here, the glucose can be used as energy. This happens faster when you eat simple sugars, so you feel hungry again sooner. Complex sugars provide energy for a longer time, making you feel full longer.

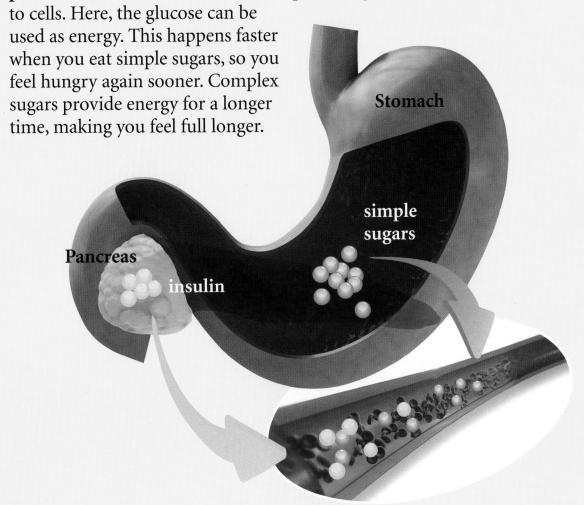

Stomach

simple sugars

Pancreas

insulin

Are You Being Served?

Eating the right foods and enough of them each day will help you get the vitamins and nutrients you need to stay in great shape. Children ages 4 to 13 should have 4 to 6 servings of grains daily.

Cookies and cakes are a delicious treat. Although they are made from grains, they have great deal of sugar and high calories. These foods should only be eaten as a special snack.

Try using the foods below to plan a daily serving of grains. Then, mix and match grain products to prepare your grain servings for one week.

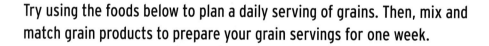

1 slice of rye, white, or pumpernickel bread (35 grams)

1/2 pita bread (35 grams)

1/2 cup cooked pasta (125 mL)

1/2 bagel (34 grams)

1/2 whole grain muffin (35 grams)

Counting Servings in a Meal

Check out the servings in a meal with fresh bread, chicken, vegetables, a glass of milk, and an orange for dessert.

250 mL (1 cup) vegetables	➤ **2 Fruit & Vegetables** Food Guide Servings
125 mL chicken breast	➤ **1 Meat & Alternatives** Food Guide Servings
1 slice rye bread	➤ **1 Grain Products** Food Guide Servings
250 mL 1% milk	➤ **1 Milk & Alternatives** Food Guide Servings
1 orange	➤ **1 Fruit & Vegetables** Food Guide Servings

1 bowl of cold cereal (30 grams)

1 bowl of hot cereal (150 grams)

2 cups plain popcorn (500 mL)

1/2 cup cooked wild, white, or brown rice (34 grams)

1 small whole wheat waffle (35 grams)

Fitness Fun

Healthy eating is just part of keeping your body in top form. In Canada, more than 50 percent of boys and 60 percent of girls do not get enough physical activity. From walking to playing team sports or riding a bike, there are many ways to get the physical activity you need each day.

It is recommended that children take part in at least 90 minutes of physical activity each day. This may include playing a sport, walking a dog, or practising yoga.

Food and Fitness Facts

Walking for 22 minutes will burn
half of a doughnut.

Thirty minutes of climbing stairs burns a
small serving of French fries.

Spending 13 minutes on a bike burns
off a glass of pop.

It takes 18 minutes of gardening to
burn off 25 peanuts.

WORK ON THIS
If you ate a doughnut, fries, and a pop today, how much would you have to work out to burn off those calories so that you did not gain weight?

Answer: 65 minutes

Calories and Consumption
Your body needs energy to operate. Food provides this energy. A calorie is a unit of energy. Calories are used to measure the amount of potential energy foods have if they are used by your body. A gram of carbohydrates or protein has 4 calories, while a gram of fat contains 9 calories. Your body needs a certain amount of calories each day to function well. If you eat fewer calories than your body requires, you may lose weight. If you eat more calories, you may gain weight. To maintain your weight, you need to burn as many calories as you eat. To burn calories, you need to do physical activity.

Time to Dine

Granola Goodness

What you will need

1 cup quick-cooking oats

0.5 cup shredded coconut

0.5 cup pecans

0.25 cup honey

0.25 cup margarine

1.5 teaspoons cinnamon

a handful of raisins

Mixing bowl

Wooden spoon

Large pan

Chopping knife

What to do

1. Melt the margarine in a microwave.
2. With an adult's help, chop the pecans.
3. Mix the oats, coconut, chopped pecans, honey, melted margarine, and cinnamon in a bowl.
4. Place the mixture in the baking pan. Put the pan in the oven, and let cook for 25 to 30 minutes at 350 degrees Fahrenheit.
5. Remove from the oven, and let cool. Pour the raisins onto the mixture, and enjoy.

Baking Bread

What you will need

10 ounces of
  raspberries
2 tablespoons of
  raspberry jam
2 eggs
0.75 cup of oil

1.5 cups of flour
0.5 teaspoons of
  baking soda
1 cup sugar
1.5 teaspoons of
  cinnamon

Dash of salt
Blender
Wooden spoon
Mixing bowl
Loaf pan

What to do

1. Blend the raspberries and the jam until smooth.
2. Mix the flour, sugar, cinnamon, and baking soda
   in a bowl. Then, add the eggs, oil, and blended
   raspberries. Stir well.
3. Grease the loaf pan, and pour the mixture inside.
4. Place the pan in the oven, and bake at 350 degrees
   Fahrenheit for 50 to 60 minutes. Remove from the
   oven, let cool, and enjoy.

What Have You Learned?

What is added to
some breads to
make them
brown in colour?

Answer: molasses

What are the four
food groups?

Answer:
Fruit and Vegetables
Milk and Alternatives
Meat and Alternatives
Grain Products

What are the three
parts of the kernel?

Answer: Bran, germ,
and endosperm

How can you burn
off half a doughnut?

Answer:
Walk for 22 minutes

What is gluten?

Answer: A tough, elastic
protein found in grains

What are two
categories of grains?

Answer:
Refined and whole

Further Research

How can I find out more about grains and healthy eating?

Most libraries have computers that connect to a database that contains information on books and articles about different subjects. You can input a key word and find material on that person, place, or thing you want to learn more about. The computer will provide you with a list of books in the library that contain information on the subject you searched for. Non-fiction books are arranged numerically, using their call number. Fiction books are organized alphabetically by the author's last name.

Websites

For a copy of Canada's Food Guide, surf to
www.hc-sc.gc.ca/fn-an/food-guide-aliment/index-eng.php.

To learn more about healthy living, download the guide at
www.healthycanadians.gc.ca/pa-ap/cg-cg_e.html.

For information about your body, fitness, food and other health topics, visit
http://kidshealth.org/kid.

Glossary

antioxidants: substances that help remove toxins from the body

bran: the outer layer of grain that is left after the grain is ground and sifted

calories: units of measure for the amount of heat made by a food when it is used by the body

carbohydrates: compounds made of carbon, hydrogen, and oxygen; sugars and starches

diabetes: a disease in which a person has too much blood sugar and needs to be given insulin

endosperm: the part of a seed that stores food for the developing plant

fats: oily substances found in plant and animal tissue

germ: the inside of a seed

minerals: natural substances that are not plants or animals

obesity: very overweight

pancreas: a large gland near the stomach that makes insulin and digestive juices

protein: a substance that is needed by all living things

vitamins: natural or humanmade substances that keep the body healthy

Index